YOUR KNOWLEDGE HAS VALUE

Bibliographic information published by the German National Library:

The German National Library lists this publication in the National Bibliography;
detailed bibliographic data are available on the Internet at http://dnb.dnb.de .

Imprint:

Copyright © 2016 GRIN Verlag, Open Publishing GmbH
Print and binding: Books on Demand GmbH, Norderstedt Germany
ISBN: 9783668335233

This book at GRIN:

http://www.grin.com/en/e-book/342695/ecosystem-dynamics-in-paluma-and-crystal-creek-rainforest

Kassidy-Rose McMahon

Ecosystem Dynamics In Paluma and Crystal Creek Rainforest

GRIN Publishing

GRIN - Your knowledge has value

Since its foundation in 1998, GRIN has specialized in publishing academic texts by students, college teachers and other academics as e-book and printed book. The website www.grin.com is an ideal platform for presenting term papers, final papers, scientific essays, dissertations and specialist books.

Visit us on the internet:

http://www.grin.com/

http://www.facebook.com/grincom

http://www.twitter.com/grin_com

ECOSYSTEM DYNAMICS

PALUMA AND CRYSTAL CREEK RAINFOREST

MCMAHON, KASSIDY-ROSE

The special life forms of three separate locations in the rainforest were observed and recorded to determine the impact of deforestation on the biotic and abiotic factors of the rainforest ecosystem. It was found that many of the special life forms that existed in the unlogged area of the rainforest were absent in the partially logged forest. It was also noted that the abiotic components of the sites, including the temperature, wind speed, humidity, light reading and weather conditions were vastly different. The data was very useful, but was only representative of three sites at one location. The data was based on estimation rather than exact values, which reduced the accuracy and reliability. Finally, it was decided that 1000m^2 of Paluma Range National Park should not be cleared because of the ecological impacts and the economic and educational consequences.

Content

1.0 Introduction

Paluma and Crystal Creek Rainforest Development Proposal

In an attempt to increase the number of students that can camp on site and learn about the rainforest, the Paluma Environmental Education Centre (PEEC) is considering an expansion of its current location. The suggested plans require the removal of approximately 1000m^2 of Paluma Range National Park and will double the capacity of students able to stay in cabins. However, the Paluma Range National Park contains various special life forms of flora and fauna, which must be preserved in the best interest of the natural ecosystem. It is therefore recommended that no land is to be cleared and that further action be taken to preserve the rainforest. The major points that will be covered within the report are the environmental and educational impacts of clearing an area of the rainforest to justify the decision made.

2.0 Methodology

The primary data that was compiled in a fieldtrip log book and was collected from three sites of Paluma and Crystal Creek Rainforest: an open Eucalypt forest (site 1), an unlogged forest (site 2) and a selectively logged forest (site 3). The biotic (special life forms) and abiotic (weather conditions, temperature, humidity, wind speed, light reading) factors of the three sites were recorded in the logbook and analysed in the 'Analysis of Primary Data' section of this report. The secondary data was sourced from a range of websites, which was critically evaluated in the 'Annotated Bibliography' section of this report.

2.1 Analysis of Methodology

The primary data was partially reliable because the recordings were taken over two days with fairly similar weather conditions, the observations were confirmed by a group of 9 students and proper equipment (clinometer, lux meter, data logger) was used. Some issues that may have decreased the accuracy of the data was the difference in the time allowed for the average speed to be recorded, different heights where light readings were taken and different opinions on weather conditions. To improve the accuracy, and therefore the reliability, it is recommended that a specific time be set for the wind speed recording (eg. 1 minute), a set height be set for light reading (eg. 1m) and clear definitions be set for weather conditions (eg. % cloud coverage). Though the data may not have been completely accurate, it is definitely still useful to compare the three sites to determine the impact of selective logging.

3.0 Field Study Data Analysis

Site 1
Temperature	23.3°C
Humidity	67.5%
Light	3540lux
Wind speed	1.6km/hr

Site 1 had the warmest temperature, lowest humidity, highest light reading and highest wind speed compared to Site 2 and Site 3. Site 1 was an open Eucalypt forest; the canopy was sparse, meaning that the trees were not closely compacted. The sparseness of the canopy caused the higher wind speed because the trees could not form a windbreak. "Windbreaks are barriers used to reduce and redirect wind. The reduction in wind speed behind a windbreak modifies the environmental conditions or microclimate in the sheltered zone" (Brandle and Finch, n.d). The sparseness of the canopy also meant that more light could filter into the forest, which caused the high light reading. This statement is supported by a study conducted by Christine Parker into the light characteristics in open-forests, which concluded that; "More light reaches the forest floor when there is an open canopy than when the canopy is closed," (Parker, 1996). The low humidity was a result of the high temperature because of the movement of water molecules in the atmosphere. When the atmosphere is hot, the water molecules move rapidly and are spread so far apart that they are invisible, but when the temperature is lower they do not move as much, forcing them to stick and become visible. (Goldstein, 2002). If an area similar to this site were to be cleared, the canopy would become even sparser as there would be fewer trees. This would increase the light and therefore the temperature, and as the temperature increase the humidity would decrease. The removal of the trees would further increase the wind speed through the area. These changes to the abiotic factors would have significant impacts on the biotic components.

The types of biota, which were present at Site 1, were grasses (3) and ferns (2-3). The qualitative ranking system, which was used to estimate the population of species was an arbitrary scale from 0-3, where 0 was absent, 1 was rare, 2 was occasional and 3 was common. The arbitrary scale gave a quick estimation on how common different species were in the site, but did not calculate the exact number of species (quantitative). This system meant that the whole site could be included in the survey, meaning that the data was more representative, but the accuracy was reduced because of estimation. The fern has specific abiotic requirements for it to survive and reproduce, including, moisture in the air, protection from wind and protection from too much sunlight (Aone, 1998). If this site were cleared, it is predicted that the increased temperature, decreased moisture in the air (humidity) and increased wind speed would threaten the fern species.

Site 2
Temperature   22.0°C
Humidity   74.0%
Wind speed   Less than 1km/hr
Light reading   40lux

Site 2 had a cooler temperature than site 1, and therefore a higher humidity, as a result of evapotranspiration. The process of evapotranspiration combines two simultaneous processes, which release moisture into the air; these are known as evaporation and transpiration. "During evaporation, water is converted from liquid to vapour and evaporates from soil, lakes, rivers and even pavement. During transpiration, water that was drawn up through the soil by the roots evaporates from the leaves" (Trimarchi, 2008). Evapotranspiration releases moisture into the atmosphere, which consequently lowers the air temperature and reduced air pollutants (Trimarchi, 2008). Site 2 is unlogged and has a very dense canopy, meaning the trees are very close together, overlapping in fact. The denseness of the canopy means that the amount of light entered the forest is significantly reduced, which consequently increases the moisture. Butler supports this statement, "The rainforest floor is often dark and humid due to constant shade from the canopy's leaves" (Butler, 2004). The canopy acts as a windbreak, which caused the wind speed to not be recognised by the equipment. These abiotic conditions allowed for diverse biotic species to grow in the rainforest. The constant shade of the rainforest floor is essential for the functioning of the forest ecosystem, as this is where decomposition takes place. "Decomposition is the process by which fungi and microorganisms break down dead plants and animals and recycle essential materials and nutrients" (Butler, 2004). By clearing this area, the process of decomposition would be disrupted, meaning that materials and nutrients cannot be recycles, which causes an imbalance in the ecosystem.

The species found in Site 2 were noted with the same arbitrate scale: Feather Leaf Tree Palm (3), Tree Fern (3), Palm Liane (3), Pandan Liane (2), Robust Woody Liane (3), Slender Wiry Liane (2), Strangler Fig (2), Vascular Epiphytes in tree crowns (3), Non-vascular Epiphytes down low (2), Ferns (3), and thorns/prickles (3). These species require the dark, damp and fairly cool conditions to survive and compete with other species for resources, such as light. If some of the abiotic conditions were altered, as a result of clearing, the weaker species would not survive, and so the remaining species are predicted to dominate the forest. The domination of select species decreases the biodiversity of an area and threatens other species that rely on a well-balanced ecosystem. For instance, the Slender Wiry Lianes rely on tall trees to wrap their roots around as they spiral to the top of the canopy to reach the sunlight. If the Liane is unable to climb towards the sunlight, it cannot undertake Photosynthesis to make food for itself and can no longer respire, causing the elimination of this species from the ecosystem (SRL, n.d.). A section of the rainforest cannot be cleared because the abiotic conditions would be altered and many native species rely on these abiotic conditions to survive. By clearing a section of the rainforest, the process of decomposition would also be affected, which limits the resources available to species and disrupts the functioning of the entire ecosystem.

Site 3
Temperature   19.0°C
Humidity   81.0%
Wind speed   Less than 1km/hr
Light reading   188lux

Site 3 had the lowest temperature and therefore the highest humidity, which follows the trend in all 3 sites. The trend identifies that "If the amount of water vapour in the air increases, the relative humidity increases, and if the amount of water vapour in the air decreases, the relative humidity decreases" (NC State University, 2013). While humidity is dependent on the water vapour in the air, it is also affected by the air temperature, as noticed at all 3 sites, and supported by NC State University. "If the water vapour content stays the same and the temperature drops, the relative humidity increases. If the water vapour content stays the same and the temperature rises, the relative humidity decreases. This is because colder air doesn't require as much moisture to become saturated as warmer air" (NC State University, 2013). The canopy of Site 3 was fairly dense because the area was partially, but not completely logged. This meant that more light was present than Site 2 because there were some openings in the canopy, but not as much light as Site 1 because the canopy at Site 1 was much more sparse. There is a clear relationship between light and canopy coverage, as supported by the Offwell Woodland and Wildlife Trust, "The closer trees are to each other, the more their individual leaf   canopies will overlap and the less light will be able to filter through to the ground" (Offwell Woodland and Wildlife Trust, n.d.).

None of the special life forms in site 1 were found in site 3, but both site 2 and site 3 contained Tree palms (feather leaf), trees ferns, Palm Lianes, Robust Woody Lianes, Slender wiry Lianes, strangler figs, thorn/prickles, buttresses and coppice. Epiphytes were found at the Site 2 but not at Site 3, perhaps because the unlogged site was warmer. Epiphytes prefer warmer climates because temperature is linked to light. More direct sunlight is advantageous to Epiphytes because they require direct sunlight for the process of Photosynthesis. This statement is support by Butler, "Their epiphytic way of life gives these plants advantages in the rainforest, allowing them access to more direct sunlight, a greater number of canopy animal pollinators, and the possibility of dispersing their seeds via wind" (Butler, 2004). 1000m^2 of the rainforest should not be cleared because the native plant species in the rainforest rely on the abiotic components regulated by the canopy. The removal of this canopy would decrease the biodiversity and could lead to the endangerment or extinction of native species.

4.0 Consequences

4.1 Environmental

"It is estimated that within 100 years there will be no rainforests" (Conserve Energy Future, 2016). It is important to preserve rainforests to reduce greenhouse gas emission, prevent soil erosion, floods and climatic imbalance, and to prevent the extinction of native flora and fauna. When trees are removed, the amount of Carbon Dioxide increases because Photosynthesis can no longer occur. "Photosynthesis filters carbon dioxide gases out the air and releases oxygen" (Green Garage, 2015). Without this process, green houses gases build up and contribute to global warming. When trees are dug up or bulldozed from the ground, soil erosion and salinity occurs as a result. "The effects of soil erosion go beyond the loss of fertile land. It has led to increased pollution and sedimentation in streams and rivers, clogging these waterways and causing declines in fish and other species. And degraded lands are also often less able to hold onto water, which can worsen flooding (WWF, 2016). When a habitat is cleared, the native flora and fauna species are forced to migrate of they die. Often, species that do manage to migrate cannot adapt to a new environment and also die. The loss of habitat and flowing consequences of deforestation are reasons why 1000m^2 of land should not be cleared.

4.2 Educational

One advantage of removing a section of the rainforest to build more accommodation is the increase in the number of students who can camp at PEEC to learn about the rainforest. By inviting more school and University students into the rainforest, students can experience the wonder of nature and understand the important of preserving its natural beauty. By being able to accommodate more students, the future generations are empowered to protect the Paluma Range National Park and other National Parks in Australia. This is important to educate people about the need to protect endangered species so that they do not become extinct. While this can be advantageous, it contradicts the message being conveyed to students. The message being conveyed is to reduce deforestation because of the environmental impacts, but by clearing land to make space for these facilities, a section of the rainforest needed to be cleared. This reinforces the existing message that many people do not value protecting the rainforest and this reduces the impact on the message. There are alternatives, which can be suggested to ensure that students are able to be accommodated without have a significant impact on the rainforest, which will be stated in the recommendations (Refer to 5.0 Recommendations).

5.0 Recommendations

It is strongly recommended that the rainforest is not cleared to build accommodation facilities for students because of the economical, ecological and educational factors previous discussed. Instead it is recommended, that the facilities be built in an area near the PEEC, which has already been cleared rather than removing even more of the natural rainforest. There are areas on the map of Paluma Range National Park, which are currently not being used. It is suggested that the facilities are built on this land instead, to make better use of the land that is already available. Another suggestion is to improve the accommodation facilities without actually expanding them outwards. This can be achieved by placing more bunk beds in each room, encouraging camping in tents on the grass areas and expanding upwards by making two-story buildings. Another alternative would be buying the houses located near the PEEC, clearing the land and building the desired facilities on these lots, to spare the rainforest.

6.0 Conclusion

In conclusion, the $1000m^2$ of Paluma Range National Park should not be cleared to build more accommodation for students visiting the PEEC. The environmental consequences of this are increased greenhouse gas emission, soil erosion, floods, climatic imbalance and the extinction of native flora and fauna species. An advantage to clearing $1000m^2$ would be the capacity to accommodate more students, but this would contradict the message being conveyed to students, which is to preserve the rainforest. Instead, there are many alternatives, which can be considered, including utilising unused spaces, expanding facilities compactly, purchasing near properties and securing camping grounds. These alternatives minimise the impact on the rainforest, while increasing the number of students who can be accommodated at the PEEC, which was the purpose of the proposal.

7.0   Annotated Bibliography

SOURCE 1: *17 Important Pros and Cons of Deforestation.* (2015). Retrieved August 19, 2016, from Green Garage:
http://greengarageblog.org/17-important-pros-and-cons-of-deforestation

The Green Garage website is an ecologically friendly blog, which posts ideas on technologies and products that have been modified so that they are more eco-friendly, including cars, boats and homes. The website focusses on the environment and discusses the human impacts, which current affect ecosystems, including rainforests. The website has many articles, which explain the advantages and disadvantages of the human impacts on different ecosystems. This particular article is titles '17 Important Pros and Cons of Deforestation' and as the title suggests, focussing on both the advantages and disadvantages of clearing some forests. The argument is very balanced because both the pros and cons were listed and explained in detail. There were 7 pros and 10 cons, which means that the article may be slightly favouring the opposing side. The intended audience of this article is the general population, which is known from the simple and concise wording, the use of dot points and the social media links. The author provides a balanced argument to readers so they can make a decision on whether deforestation should occur. The final conclusion made by the author was that there are many pros and cons, which are related to deforestation, but in the end, no final argument was made. The text is mostly reliable because there was a balanced argument, but the nature of the organisation (an environmental blog) suggested that the negative side of the argument was slightly favoured. The special features in this text are the constant referral to statistics and facts, though there are no references or citations to inform the readers of the source. This means that the source of the statistics cannot be checked, so it is possible that they may not be credible. This source is extremely relevant and useful because many justified reasons were provides for multiple arguments, and the statistics put these reasons into perspective. The strengths of this text are its balanced argument, its conciseness and use of data; the limitations are the lack of visual components, the absence of references and the failure to clear the author. The reaction from this text was that there are many impacts to be considered before clearing forests, but there are also some advantages, which must be considered as well.

SOURCE 2: *What is deforestation?* (2010). Retrieved August 19, 2016, from eSchoolToday:
http://eschooltoday.com/forests/what-is-deforestation.html

ESchoolToday was founded in 2008 with the purpose of providing free information to young people in a fun, fast and illustrative way. The website is sponsored by BusinessGhana Internet Services, which is a leading Business portal based in Ghana, Africa. There are three authors - Nii Noi Odonkor (Co-founder), Margaret Allotey-Pappoe (Co-founded) and George Asamoa Frimpong (copy, content and quality control). The respective degrees of the

9

authors were Graphic Design and Masters in Interactive Multi-Media, Communication Design and MA/MFA in Visual Communication and Design, and Art and Masters in Interactive Multi-Media. The source defines deforestation, lists reasons why human clear forest lands, compared the deforestation shares of countries, and explains forest degradation and fragmentation. While four advantages to clearing forests was stated, the website mainly discourages deforestation, as there is more evidence for this side of the argument. The intended audience for this website is primary school children, which is known from the stated purpose of the website, the use of colour of visuals, and the simplicity of the information. No final conclusion was reached by the author, as the source was mostly fact-based with very little opinion presented. The text is quite reliable because the information is supported by source 1, but the text is not entirely reliable because none of the authors actually have a degree in ecology, only is media, art and communication. The special features of the text are the mostly relevant and colourful maps, diagrams, images, charts, which support the information. This text is fairly relevant and useful because there was a balanced argument explaining why deforestation occurs and what the negative impacts of deforestation are. The strengths of this text are its conciseness and visual components; the limitations of this text are the simplicity of the information and the lack of expertise of the authors. The reaction from this website was that deforestation is an important issue, but there are a couple of benefits to removing some areas of the rainforest.

SOURCE 3: Brandle, J., & Finch, S. (n.d.). *How Windbreaks Work*. Retrieved August 19, 2016, from University of Nebraska: http://nac.unl.edu/documents/morepublications/ec1763.pdf

The authors of this document published it under the University of Nebraska-Lincoln, which is a public research University in the Midwestern United States. The first listed author, James Brandle is a Professor of Shelterbelt Ecology at the School of Natural Resources, University of Nebraska from July 1975 to present. The second listed author, Sherman Finch has published 4 works about windbreaks, which were published by the University of Nebraska-Lincoln. The authors are experiences in their field and were published by a well-respected University, which adds to their credibility. The text explains how windbreaks work, discusses windbreak characteristics and states their effect. The main argument is that windbreaks are advantageous in growing crops, raising livestock and protecting living and working areas. The intended audience of this text is people working in the agricultural and horticultural industries because the introduction and summary targets this group. The conclusions made by the authors are that the most influential characteristics of a windbreak are the height, density, orientation, length and microclimate modifications. The text is very reliable because the authors are credible, the information is presented scientifically and there are several supporting agencies of the report including the U.S. Department of Agriculture, University of Nebraska and the Institute of Agriculture and Natural Resources. Some special features of the text are the 4 tables comparing open wind speed 20mph of different species with different densities, 2 diagrams of windbreaks and 1 map of the distribution of open field wind speed. The visual features support the text and provide statistical data that is comparative and clear. This document is limited in its usefulness for my research because only a tiny bit of the information was relevant, even though it was very scientific and impressive. The strengths were the visual aids, the credibility and conciseness of the summary. The limitations were its relevance and its usefulness for this task. Overall this text is very factual and scientific but is not very relevant or useful.

SOURCE 4: K-12: http://climate.ncsu.edu/edu/k12/.humidity
What is deforestation? (2010). Retrieved August 19, 2016, from eSchoolToday: http://eschooltoday.com/forests/what-is-deforestation.html

There were 3 original creators of the website, who all have professional degrees in Meteorology. There are 14 other authors, who all have different areas of specialty and roles in the creation of the webpage. The educational standards of the authors gives credibility to the website because all authors have a tertiary degree and area of specialty. There are many authors of the website so the author of this particular cannot be traced, which means that the educational of the author/s cannot be confirmed. This text explains relative humidity, dew point and agriculture. The information is scientific; there is no argument or opinion in the text. The intended audience for the website is students from Kindergarten to Grade 12, but this particular webpage is aimed at senior students because of the advanced vocabulary and terminology. The conclusion made by the author is that humidity is an important concept and affects health, agriculture and weather. The text is fairly reliable because the author is believed to be an expert, the information is presented formally and scientifically, and there are 2 links to National Science Education Standards. A special feature of this text is the activity, which accompanies the information provided. This text is very relevant because humidity was a key abiotic factor that was explored in the task and the information was very useful. The strengths of the text are the detailed information and 3 decorative images. The limitations are the young intended audience and the uncertainty of the education of the author. Overall this text is very relevant to the task, but the reliability cannot be determined from the background given.

SOURCE 5: Trimarchi, M. (2008). *How do trees affect the weather?* Retrieved August 21, 2016, from How Stuff Works:
http://science.howstuffworks.com/nature/climate-weather/atmospheric/trees-affect-weather1.htm

The website was founded in 1998 and gas won 23 Webby Awards, 16 W3 Awards, 2 Interactive Media Awards, 18 Communicator Awards, 7 Web Marketing Association's WebAward and 46 other Awards. The author, Maria Trimarchi, is a contributing writer for the website; she has a bachelor's degree in English from Skidmore College. Skidmore College is a private, independent liberal arts college in Saratoga Springs, New York. The author does not have a science degree, which reduces her credibility, but the website itself is very credible because of the multiple awards it was won. This text is about the positive impact of trees on the climate. The main argument is that trees are essential because they lower the temperature, reduce energy usage and reduce or remove air pollutants. The intended audience is not specific because they vocabulary is not too simple or too complex and the website is known for its diversity. The text is partially reliable because the information is legitimate because of supporting background knowledge, but the low credibility of the author reduced the reliability of the text overall. One special feature of the webpage is a diagram, which labels and shows the process of evapotranspiration. This diagram supports the information provided and visually shows the process of evapotranspiration. The text is a little bit relevant because evapotranspiration relates the humidity and climate, but not all of the information is relevant to this task. The strengths are the diagram, explanation of scientific terminology and credibility of website. The limitations are the irrelevance of some parts of the text and the limited scientific knowledge of the author. Overall, some parts of this text can be used, but a lot of it is irrelevant and the information needs to be checked.

SOURCE 6: Butler, R. (2015, December 5). *The Rainforest Floor*. Retrieved August 22, 2016, from Mongabay:
http://kids.mongabay.com/elementary/005.html

Rhett Butler founded Mongabay.com in 1999 with the aim of raising interest in and appreciation of wild lands and wildlife. He serves as editor-in-chief of the web site and president of Mongabay.org, Mongabay's non-profit arm. Rhett Butler is also Mongabay's senior writer and photographer; he creates much of the site's content. In September 2014, Rhett Butler became the first journalist to win the Parker/Gentry Award. The author is very experienced in his field, which makes him very credible. This source states the conditions of a rainforest floor and explains decomposition. The information is factual; there is no opinion or argument. The intended audience is young students because of the aim of the website, simplistic wordings and abundance of photographs. The text is very reliable because the information is fairly basic, there is extensive photographic evidence and the author is credible. A special feature of the webpage is 22 photographs from the forest floor. There is very little information, but the information that is present is very relevant and useful for this task. The strengths are the visual support, brevity of information and reliability. The limitations are the young target audience and absence of external links. Overall, the text is very reliable and relevant, but the complexity is limited.

SOURCE 6: Parker, C. (1996, November 19). *Light Characteristics in Open-forest and Closed-forest Communities*. Retrieved August 23, 2016, from People HWS: http://people.hws.edu/mitchell/oz/Papers/ParkerTer.html

The author is Christine Parker; there is no information on this author, but based on the study she seems to have science experience. This source is study on the light characteristics in open-forest and closed-forest communities. There is an abstract, introduction, 3 sites, results, discussion, conclusion and 10 references. The study follows a report structure and is written scientifically, which contributes to the credibility of the author. The main argument is that it is impossible to eliminate all human impacts on the rainforest, but it is necessary to attempt to reduce the human impacts. The intended audience is the scientific community because of the technical wording and presentation of the report. The conclusion made by the author is that the characteristics of light in open and closed forest communities are very diversified but are all intricately connected with the environment. The text is very reliable because there are 10 references, the knowledge presented is extensive and 3 sites were compared. The text is a little bit relevant because light is one of the factors that was investigated, but was not a large part of the task as a whole. The strengths of the text are the scientific terminology and insightful comparison of sites. The limitations are the unknown background of the author and usefulness. Overall, the text has some relevance to the task, but only small parts can be used.

SOURCE 7: Goldstein. (2002). *Weather*. Retrieved August 24, 2016, from Info Please: http://www.infoplease.com/cig/weather/moisture-humidity.html

Mel Goldstein, Ph.D. was an on-air television meteorologist and the Chief meteorologist for WTNH television in New Haven, Connecticut from 1986-2011. The information was extracted from 'The Complete Idiot's Guide to Weather', which was published in 2002. The text is about moisture and humidity and how temperature affects humidity. The information is all scientific and there is no source of opinion. The intended audience is people who have little or no knowledge on weather, as suggested by the title of the book where he extract was taken. The text is very reliable because the author has a Doctorate in Meteorology and has extensive meteorological knowledge. There are 2 diagrams and 1 table, which support the information; the diagrams visually demonstrate the movement of water molecules and the table show the relationship between air temperature and relative humidity. The text is quite relevant because humidity and air temperature are two factors, which were examined in the task. The strengths of the source are the visual aids, credibility of author and scientific wording. The only limitation to the source is the large amount of information, which is not completely relevant to the task. Overall, this source is very reliable and quite useful.

SOURCE 8: Trust, O. W. (n.d.). *Woodlands & Biodiversity*. Retrieved August 26, 2016, from Countryside info:
http://www.countrysideinfo.co.uk/woodland_manage/woodbio.htm

The author of the website if the Offwell Woodland and Wildlife Trust. The trustees of this website are DJ Lyons, DW Tilbury, J Benfield and V Whitlock. The aim of the website is to provide a wide range of environmental education for all age and promoting conservation. The source explores woodlands and biodiversity by discussing the importance of light. There is no main argument as the source is scientific, even though the information is presented concisely. The website is aimed at all ages, but there is a slight focus on children, as shown by the conciseness of information and type of organisation. The text is mostly reliable because the authors are conservation experts and there is no obvious opinion in the text. The text is quite relevant because it discusses light, which was one of the factors explored in the task. Some of the information is very useful but other parts are not as useful. The strengths of the source are the conciseness of information and emphasis of key points.

The limitations are the unknown educational background of the authors and the absence of references. Overall, this source is quite relevant and is mostly reliable.

Bibliography

17 Important Pros and Cons of Deforestation. (2015). Retrieved August 19, 2016, from Green Garage: http://greengarageblog.org/17-important-pros-and-cons-of-deforestation

Brandle, J., & Finch, S. (n.d.). *How Windbreaks Work.* Retrieved August 19, 2016, from University of Nebraska: http://nac.unl.edu/documents/morepublications/ec1763.pdf

Butler, R. (2015, December 5). *The Rainforest Floor.* Retrieved August 22, 2016, from Mongabay: http://kids.mongabay.com/elementary/005.html

Goldstein. (2002). *Weather.* Retrieved August 24, 2016, from Info Please: http://www.infoplease.com/cig/weather/moisture-humidity.html

Humidity. (2013, August 13). Retrieved August 20, 2016, from Climate Education for K-12: http://climate.ncsu.edu/edu/k12/.humidity

Parker, C. (1996, November 19). *Light Characteristics in Open-forest and Closed-forest Communities.* Retrieved August 23, 2016, from People HWS: http://people.hws.edu/mitchell/oz/Papers/ParkerTer.html

Trimarchi, M. (2008). *How do trees affect the weather?* Retrieved August 21, 2016, from How Stuff Works: http://science.howstuffworks.com/nature/climate-weather/storms/trees-affect-weather1.htm

Trust, O. W. (n.d.). *Woodlands & Biodiversity.* Retrieved August 26, 2016, from Countryside info: http://www.countrysideinfo.co.uk/woodland_manage/woodbio.htm

What is deforestation? (2010). Retrieved August 19, 2016, from eSchoolToday: http://eschooltoday.com/forests/what-is-deforestation.html